This book is
dedicated to all whom
believe in the magic
of miracles and
friendship

Santa's Helpers Save Christmas

Written by
Natasha D'Anna

Illustrated by
Wingki Kwok

'Twas thanksgiving eve at the home of Violet and Kelly. As they sat patiently in their clubhouse waiting for the rain to stop, a sudden loud thump was heard outside. The girls looked out the door to see what it was. To their surprise a huge velvet red sack sat at the foot of the door.

The girls struggled to push the door open and hurried to pull the bag into the clubhouse. It was very heavy, and they couldn't imagine what was hidden inside.

Kelly and Violet looked at each other then at the bag. Kelly decided to open it as Violet held a flash light over.

The tightly gripped rope unraveled and out popped letters addressed to Santa clause.

Violet dropped the flashlight and immediately began helping her sister dig into the bag. The letters were addressed to Santa and they were not Santa!! What were they going to do?

The girls opened one letter to find that they were from Santa's helpers and elves. Each one included the elves family assignments and toy maker lists.

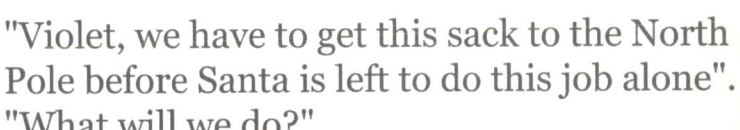

"Violet, we have to get this sack to the North Pole before Santa is left to do this job alone".
"What will we do?"
"How will we get this to the North Pole?"
Cried Kelly.

Violet decided to continue looking inside the bag for clues; when suddenly a snow globe was found at the very bottom.

She gently removed the globe and recognized the beautiful snow , Santa's workshop and an address across the front of the globe, that read "1 Believe Way, North Pole".

However will they make it there?

As the rain stopped the girls decided to go up to bed and lock the sack away in their clubhouse.

The night was long, but as they fell fast asleep they began to dream.

Violet and Kelly shared a dream of visiting the North Pole. Their twintuition lead them to Santa's workshop.

The workshop was beautiful and so full of joy. It was everything they could have imagined. The girls met with Santa and shared the news of having the velvet sack mistakenly dropped at their club house. Santa was relieved that his little visitors had found the sack, and quickly added them to the helpers list.

Violet and Kelly met many of Santa's friends including, Mrs Clause. They helped turn on the Christmas lights for the holiday ceremony and ate tons of gingerbread cookies.

Before long it was time to go and Violet and Kelly had to complete their job of getting the sack to 1 Believe Way, North Pole.

It was Violet and Kelly's job to put together a plan!

In the morning the girls rushed down to their clubhouse. To their surprise the front door was open, but their parents did not mention finding the sack. As they slowly entered they looked left and right but did not see the sack.

Kelly, do you think someone took it?! Cried Violet.

No, replied Kelly as she peeled a note from the box left on the floor, where the sack had been. It was a Thank you note from Santa addressed to "Santa's Helpers" with a special gift inside.

Violet and Kelly says one belief can make dreams come true.

WWW.tWiNdoLLiCioUS.CoM

HoLiday CoLLectioN
& bLog

Violet and Kelly would love for you to share your adventures with a best friend, sister or brother as they do in each story.

By connecting with them on their

@ Twindollicious

you may share your stories together.

Copyright © 2014 TwinDollicious Inc
PO Box 40340
Staten Island, NY 10304
United States

www.ingramcontent.com/pod-product-compliance
Lightning Source LLC
Chambersburg PA
CBHW040122170426
42811CB00125B/1516